ColorArt™
Real Men Color

new seasons®

a division of Publications International, Ltd.

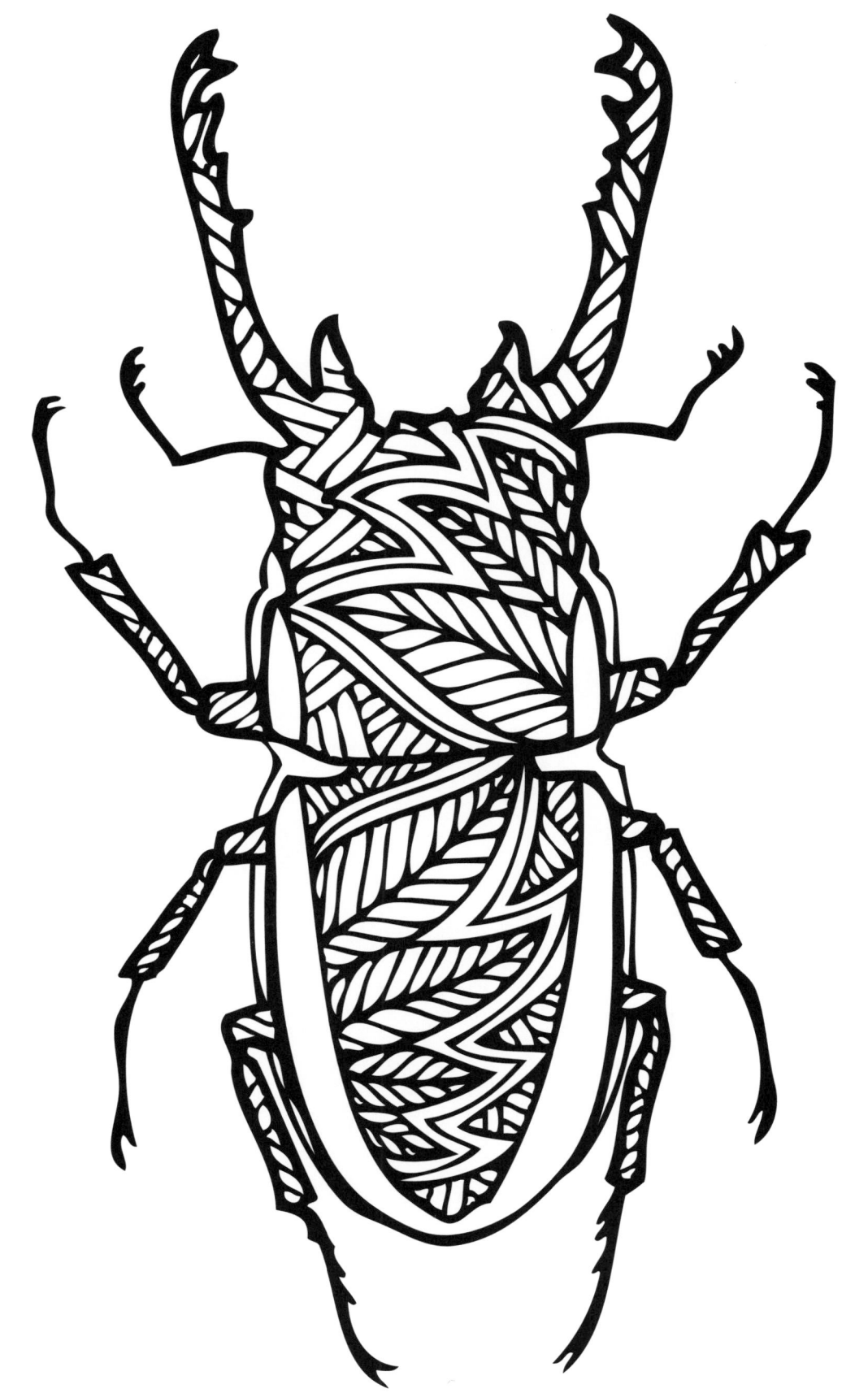

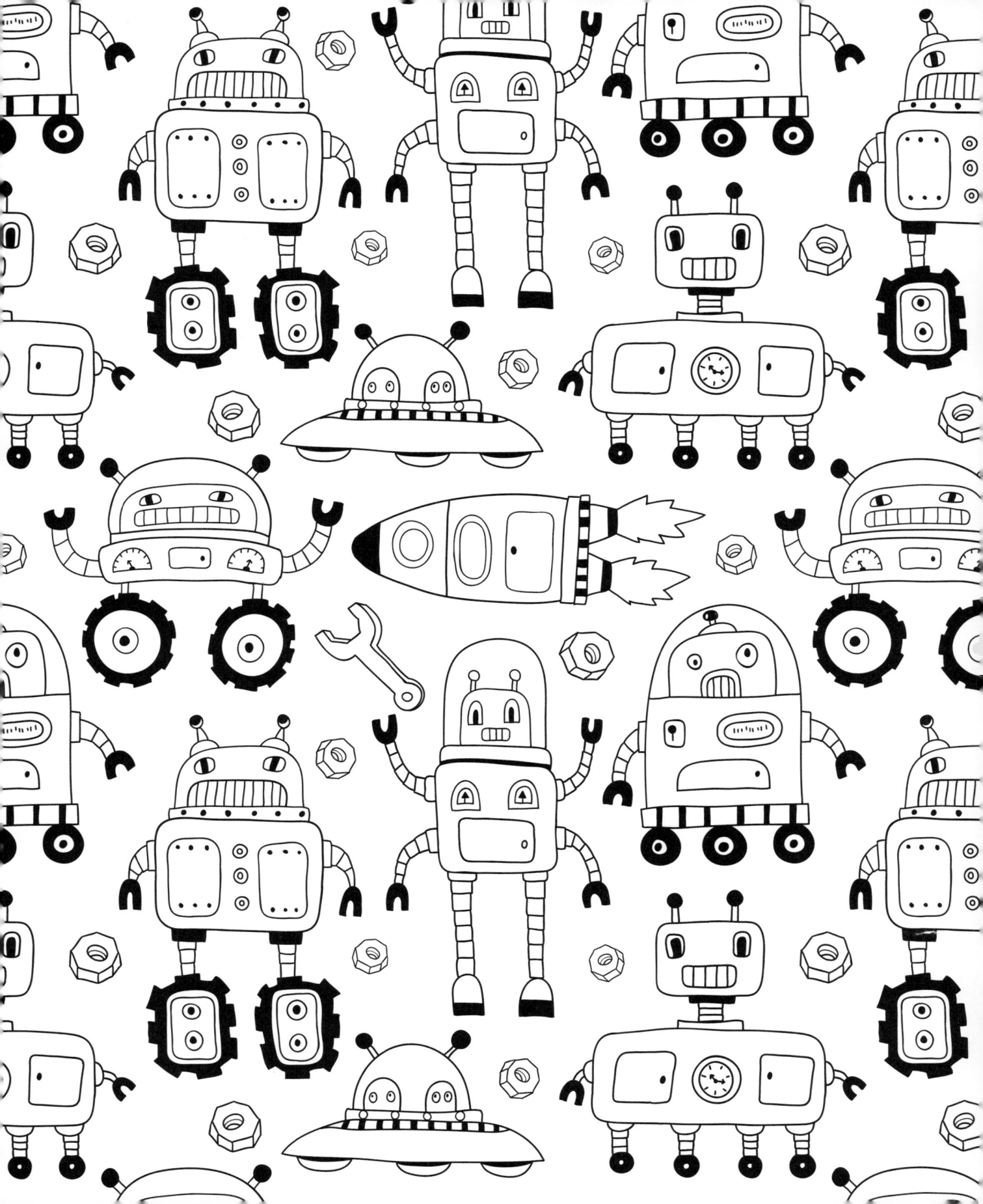

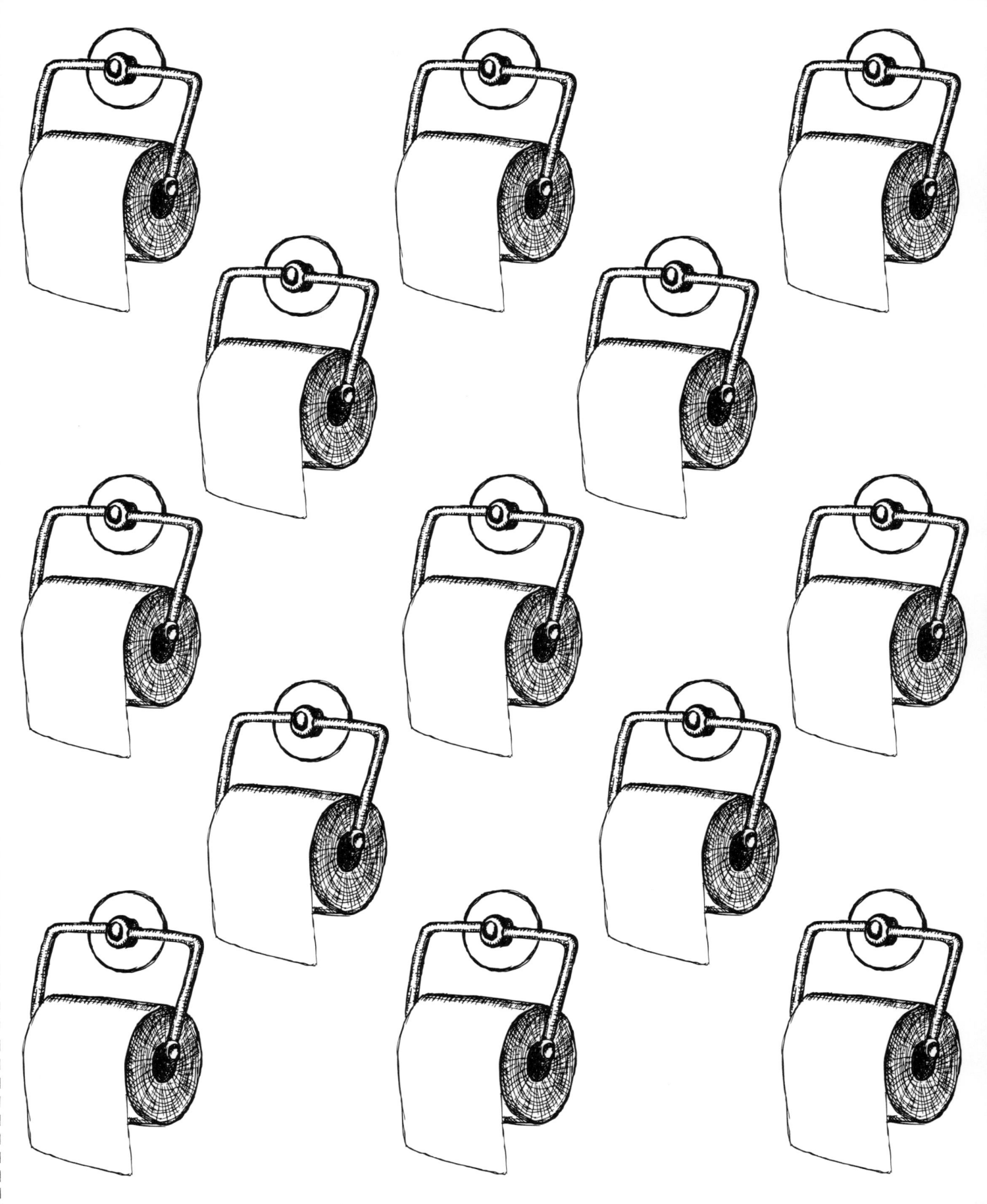

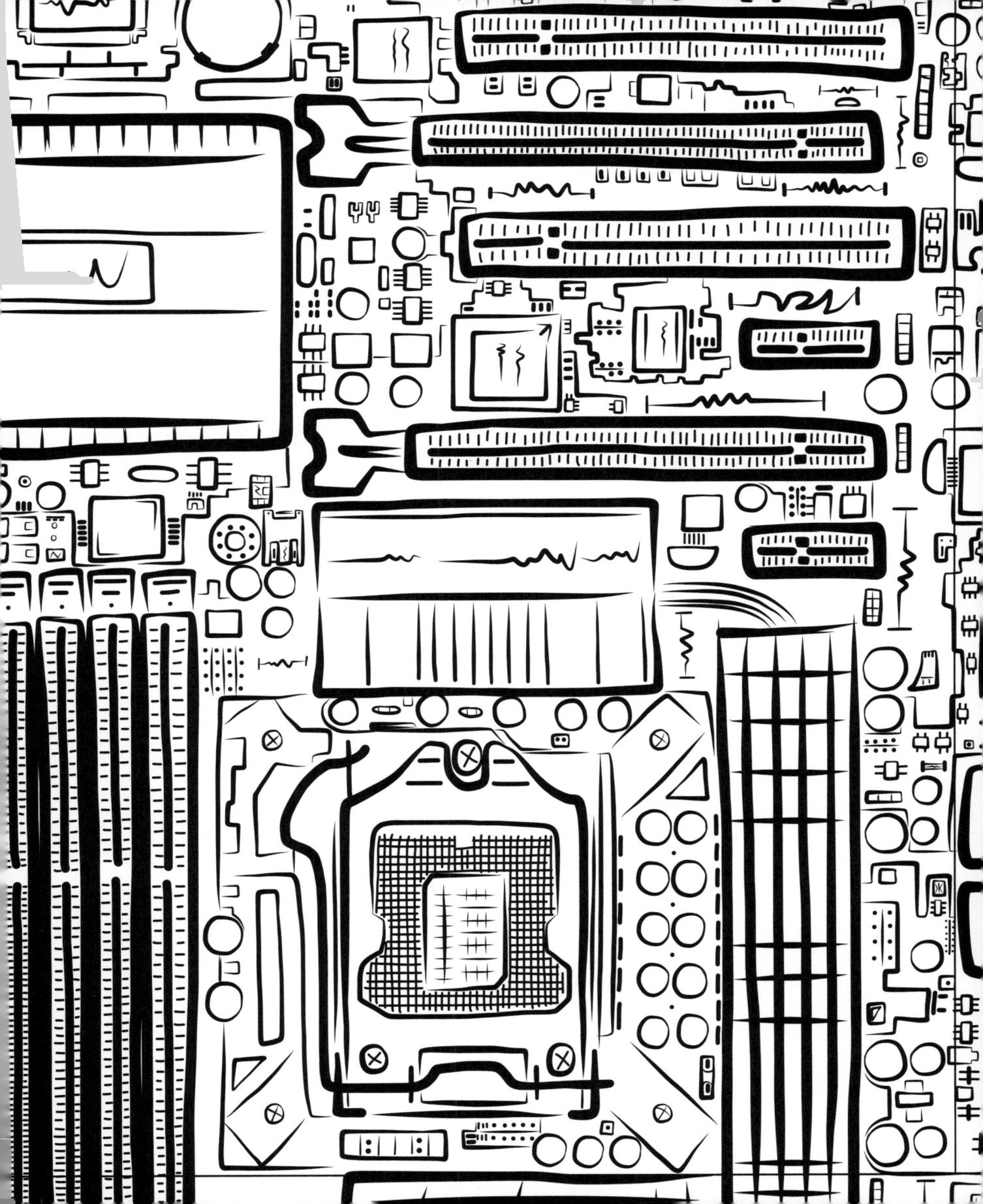

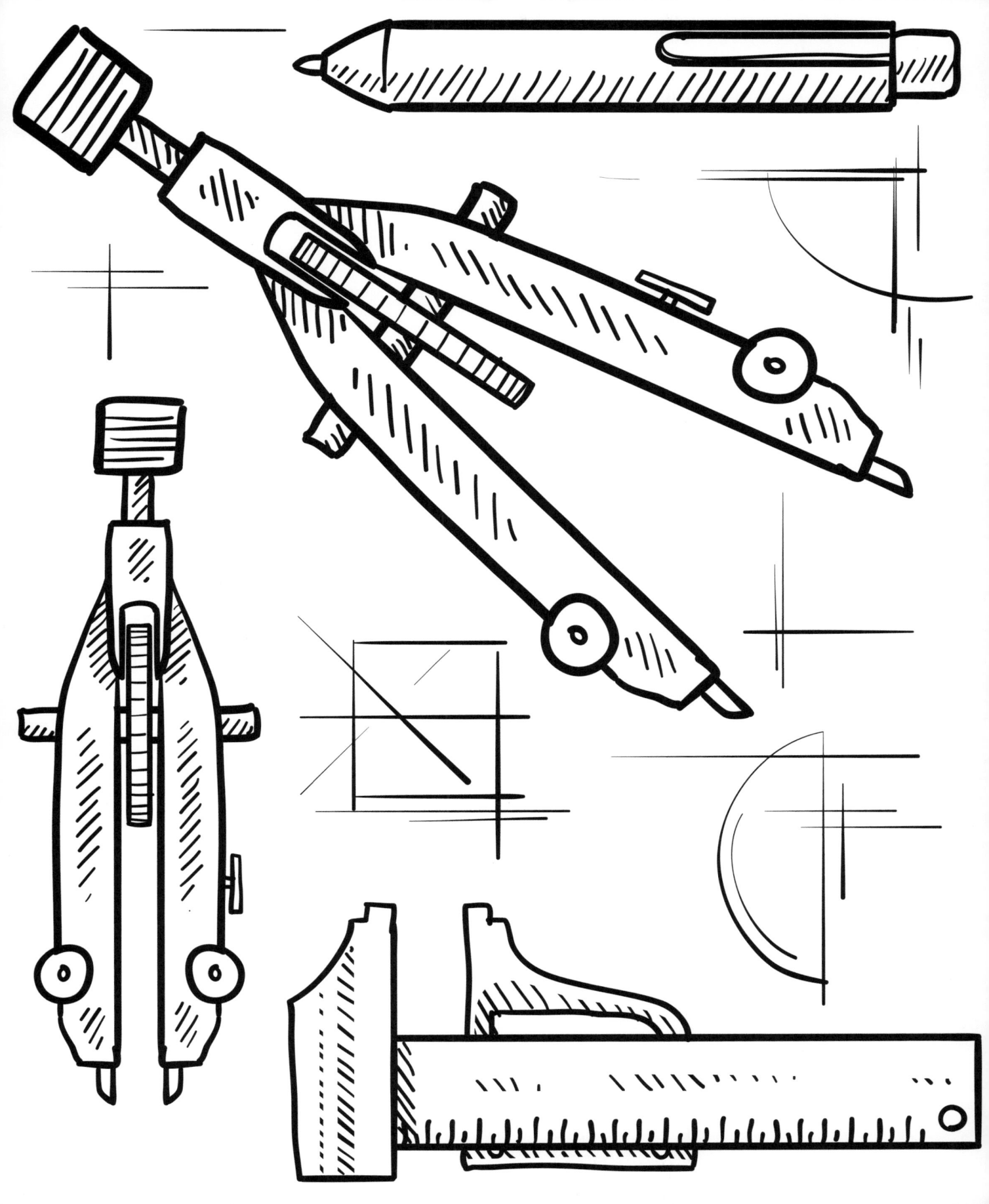

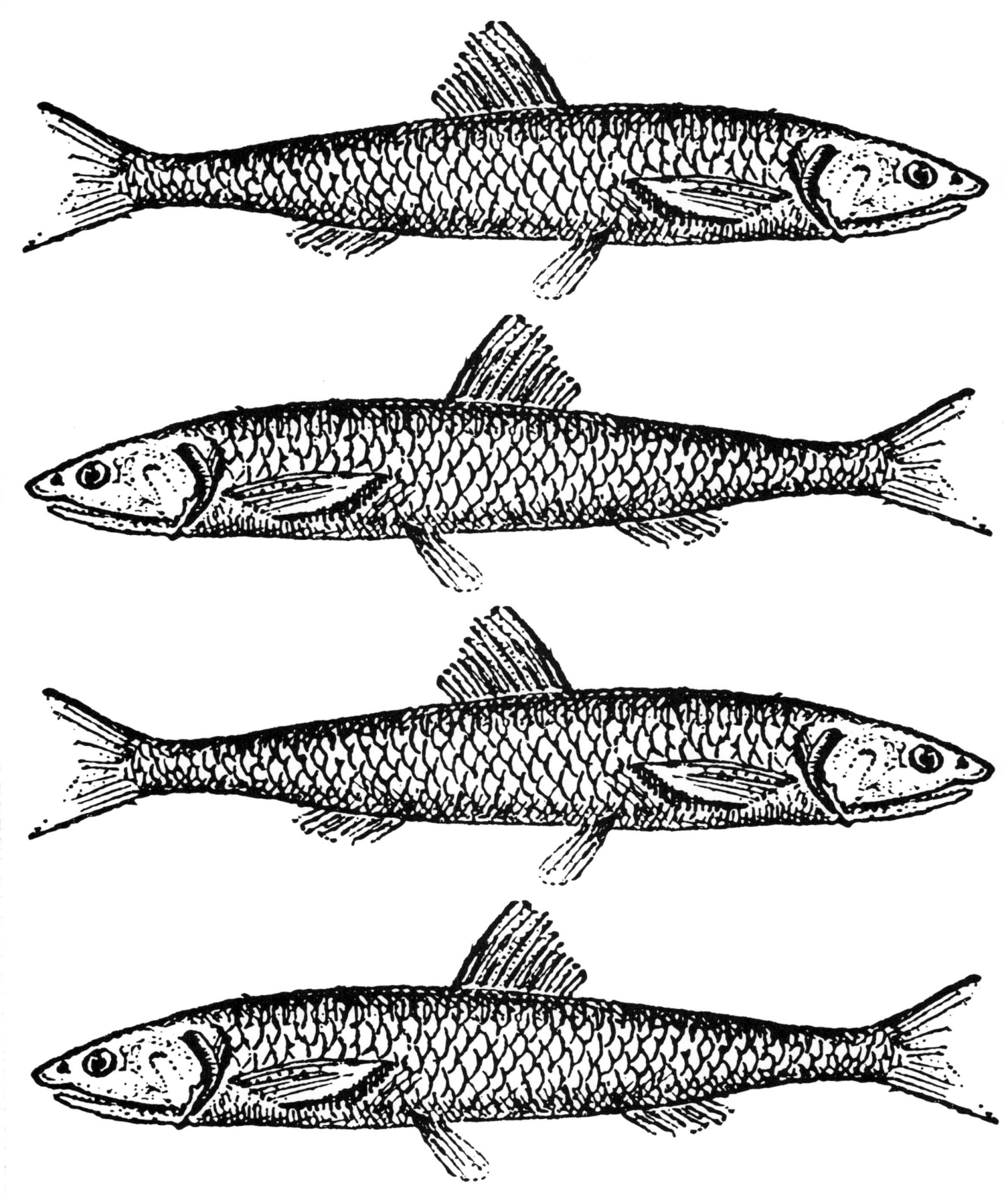

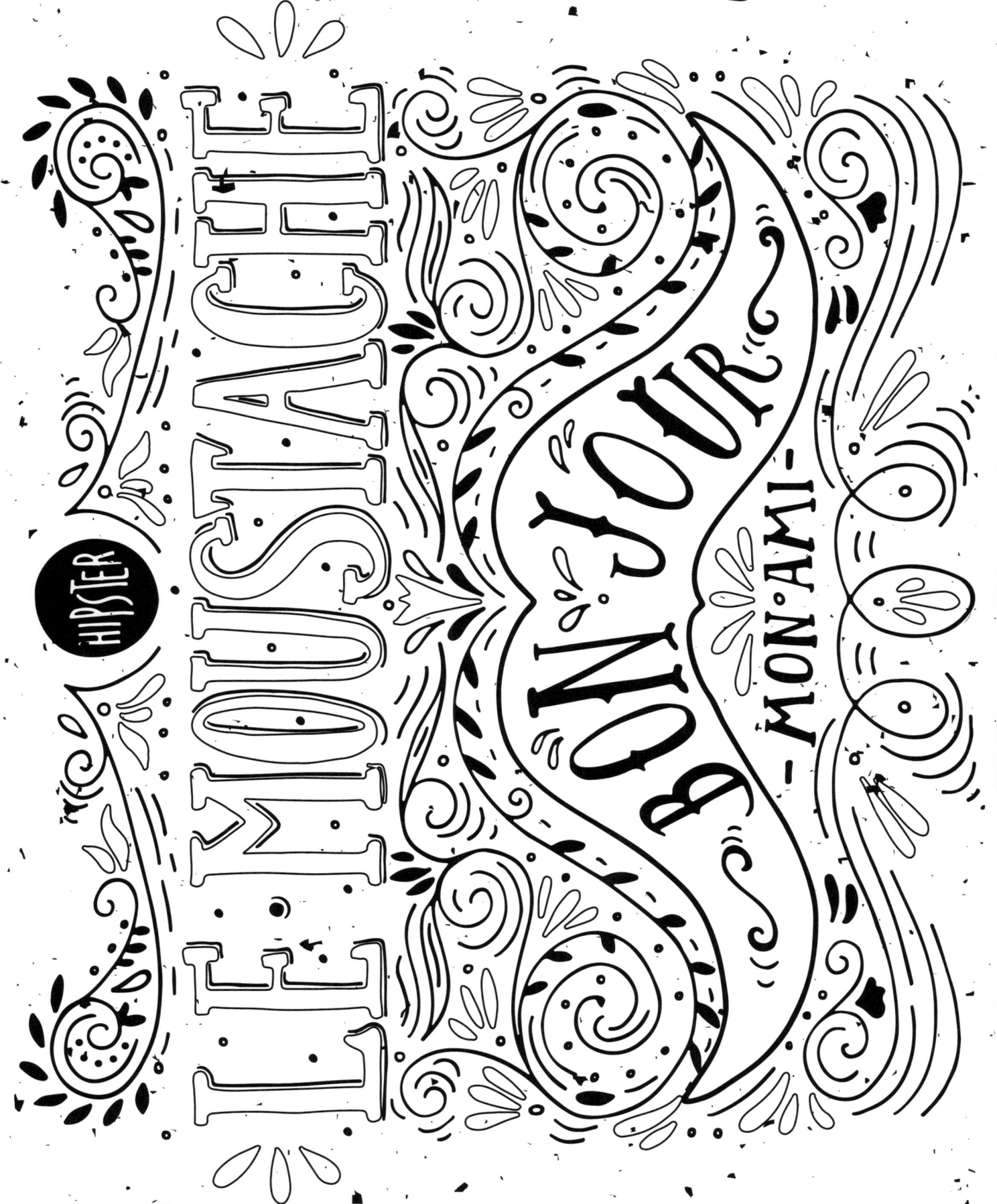

Calif.
SURF
99
Clothing
CO
LONG BOARD
TRADE MARK
BEACH
LIFE

APPAREL CO
TRUE BRAND
Beach Clothing
LONG BOARD
Surf's Up
EST. 99
CALIF.
TRADE MARK PAT. OFF
FREE WAVES?

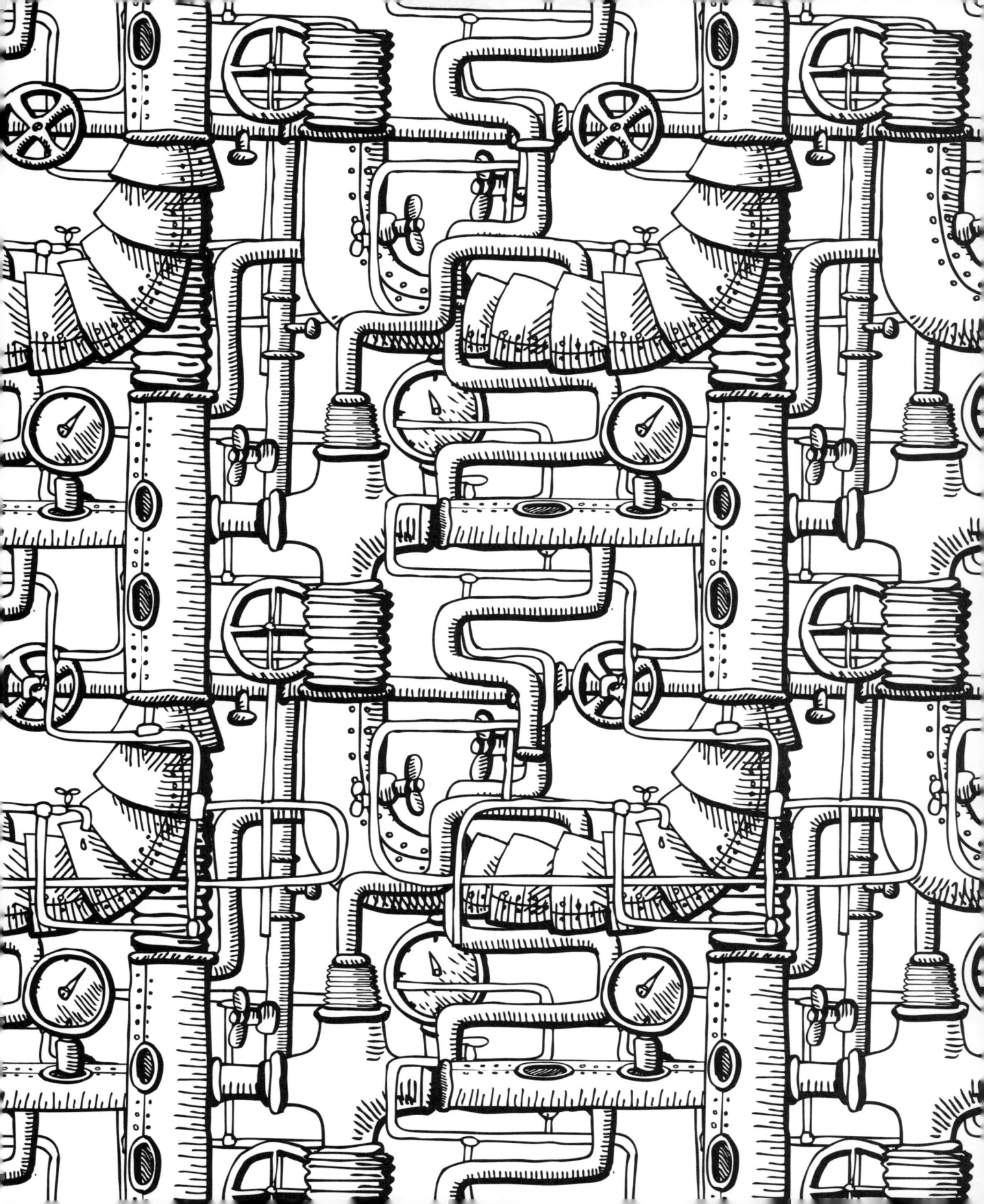

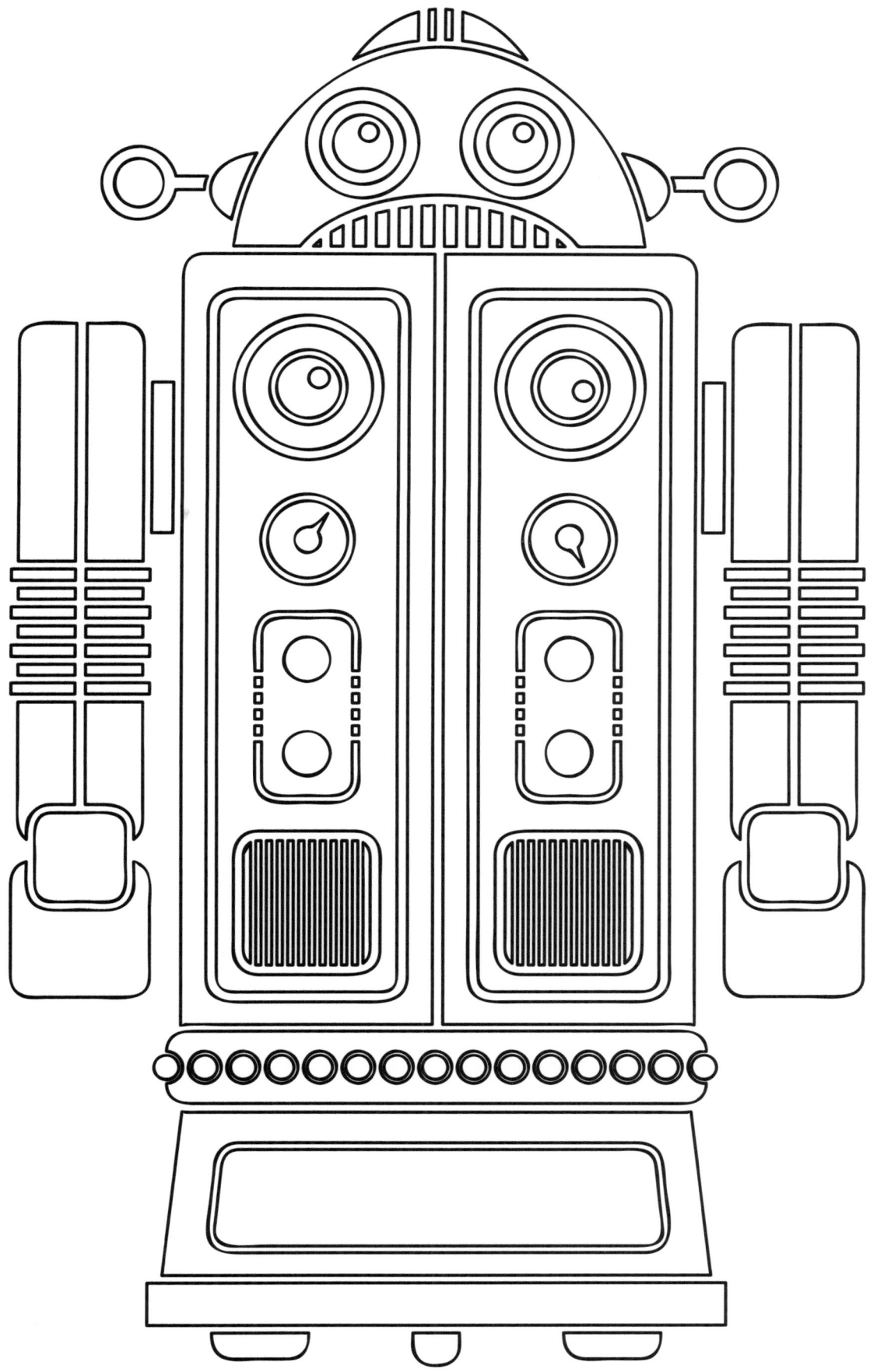

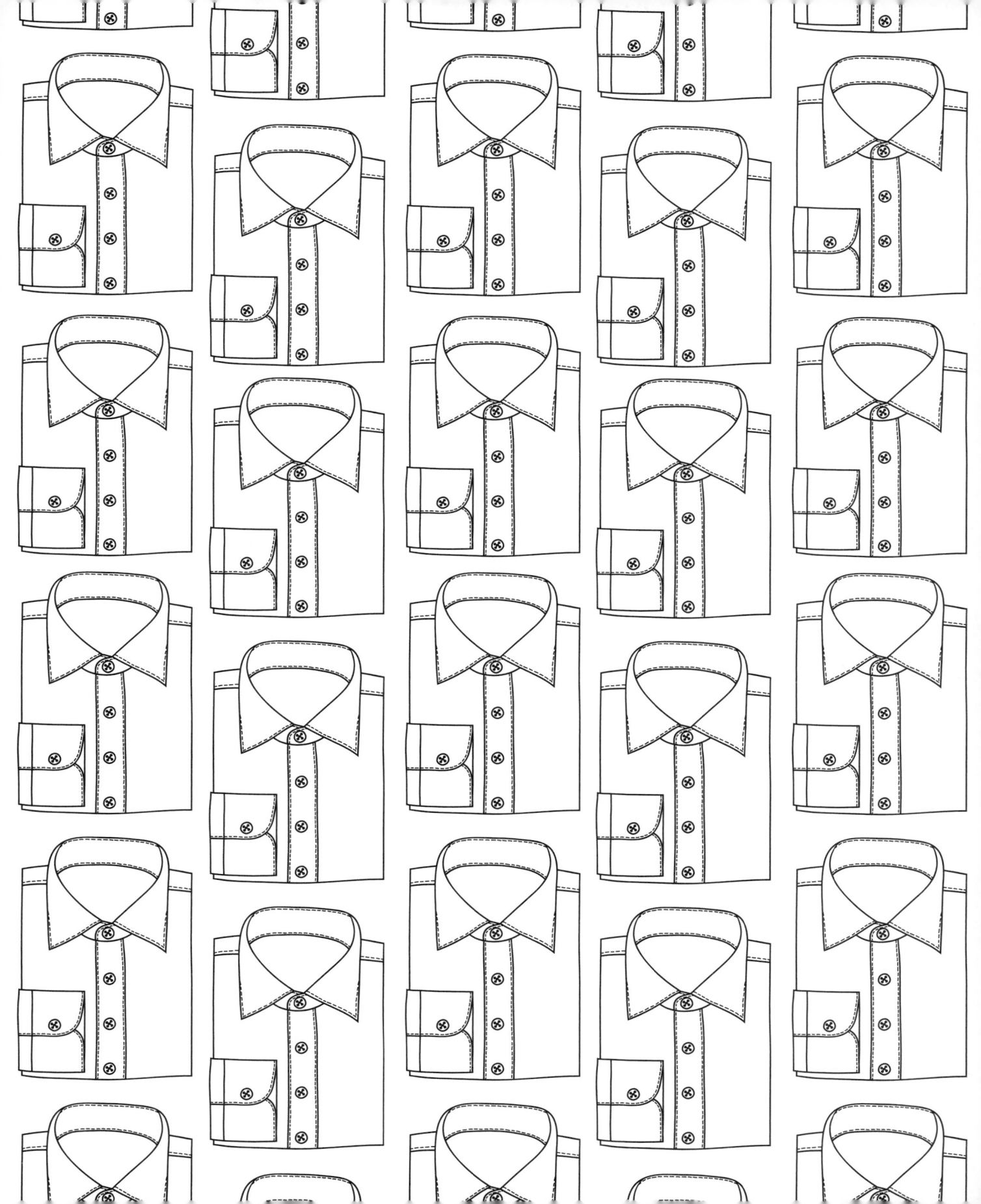

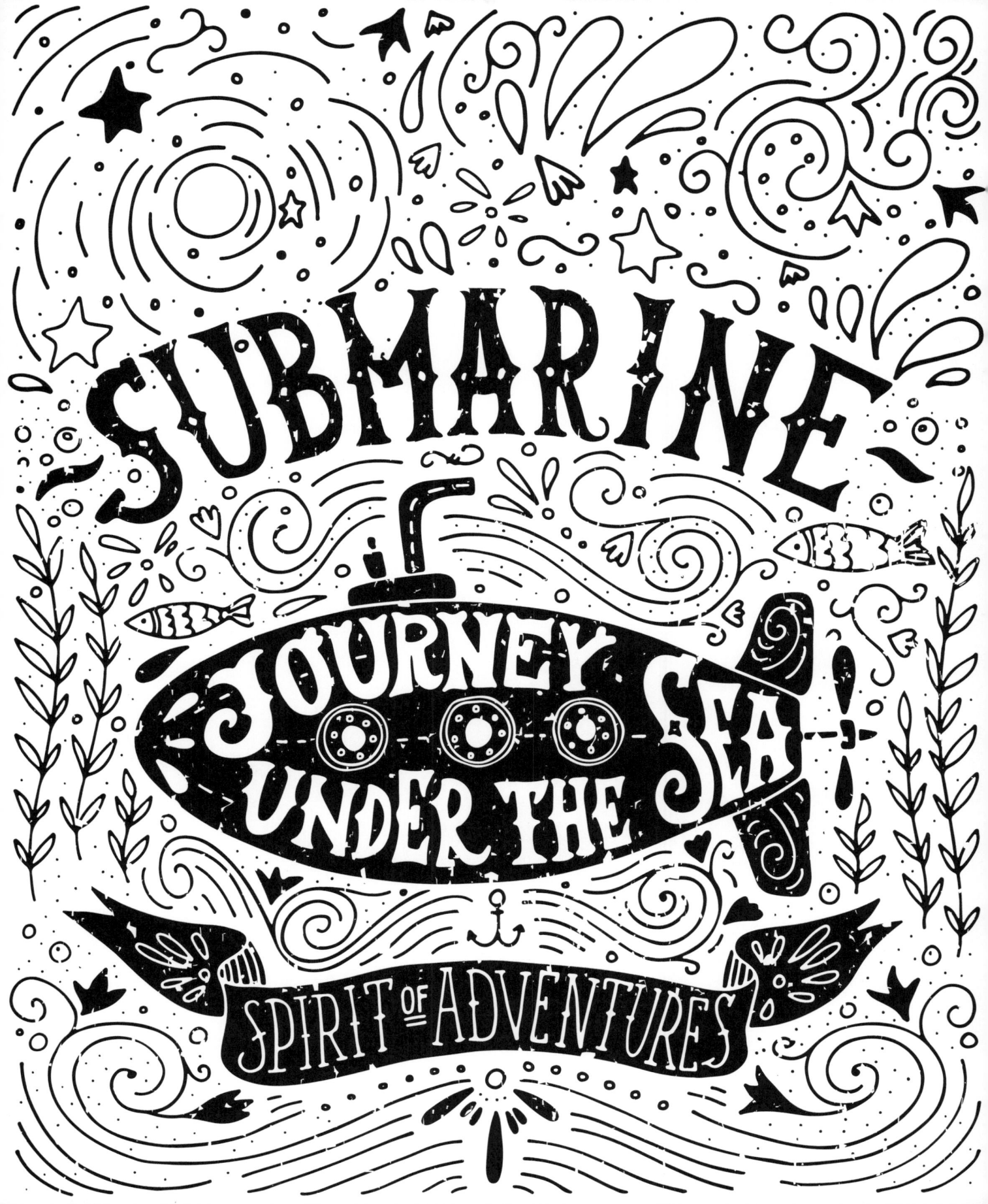

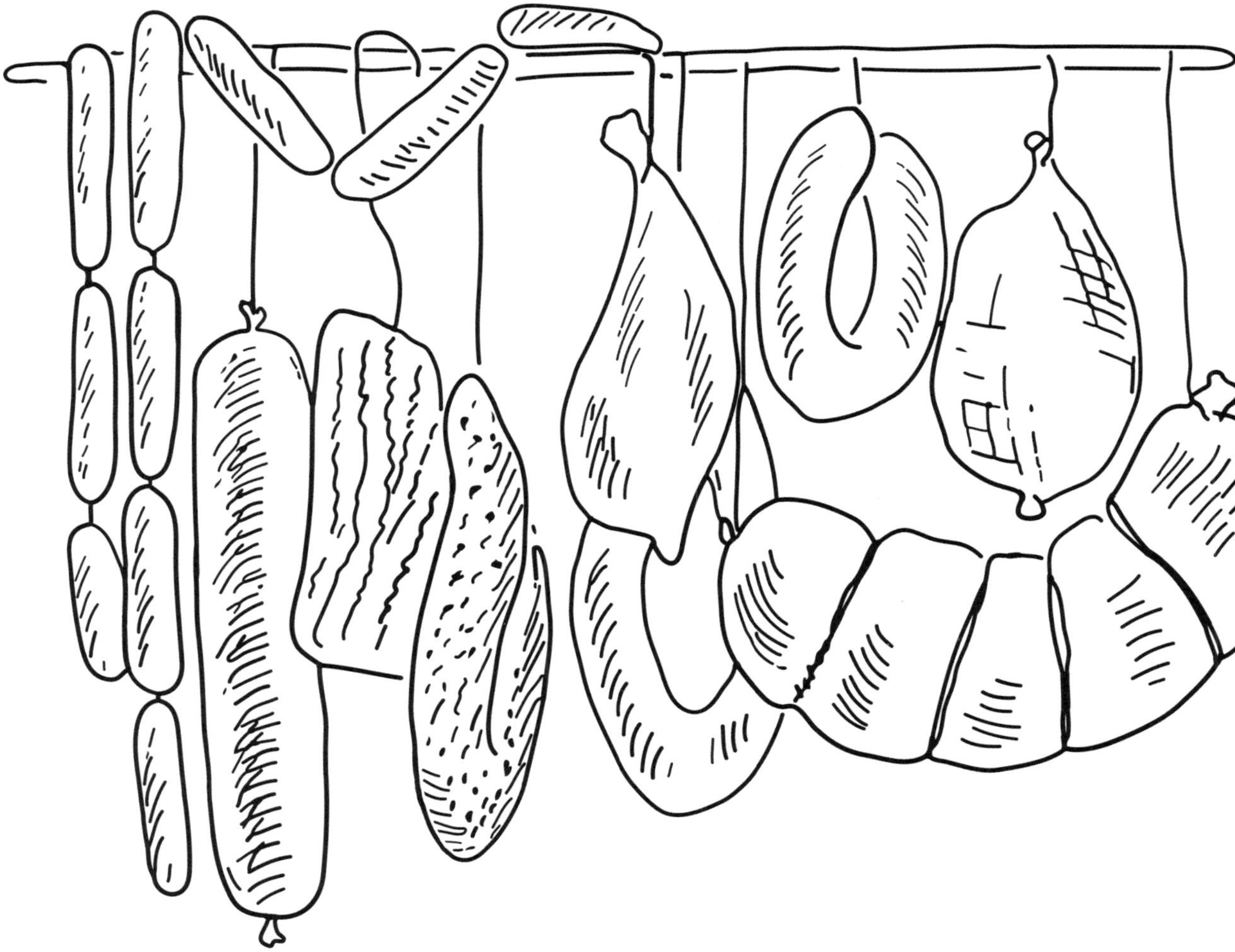